THIS CANDLEWICK BIOGRAPHY BELONGS TO:

A man has to have goals—for a day, for a lifetime—
and that was mine, to have people say, "There goes
Ted Williams, the greatest hitter who ever lived."

—Ted Williams

For my dad,
who shared his baseball cards with me
and told me about Ted Williams

THERE GOES TED WILLIAMS

The Greatest Hitter Who Ever Lived

Matt Tavares

CANDLEWICK PRESS

TABLE OF CONTENTS

CHAPTER ONE 1

CHAPTER TWO 4

CHAPTER THREE 8

CHAPTER FOUR 12

CHAPTER FIVE 16

CHAPTER SIX 22

CHAPTER SEVEN 26

CHAPTER EIGHT 30

AUTHOR'S NOTE 34

BIBLIOGRAPHY 35

STATISTICS 36

INDEX 38

AUTHOR BIOGRAPHY 40

CHAPTER ONE

The lights turn on
at the North Park playground
in San Diego, California.
The other kids leave.
They need to be home in time for dinner.
They have to go do their homework.

But not Ted Williams.
Ted Williams can stay out
as late as he wants.

All by himself, he practices his swing.
Two on, two out, last of the ninth,
he says to himself,
down three to one, two balls, two strikes,
and here's the pitch . . .

HOME RUN!

Every time.

Ted Williams wishes he wasn't so skinny.
He hates when the kids at the playground
call him Bird Legs.
He does push-ups every day.
First twenty a day, then thirty, forty,
fifty, one hundred.
He does push-ups on his fingertips.

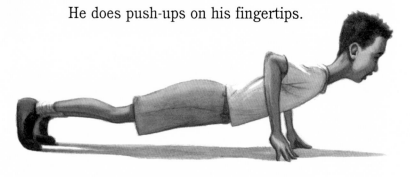

He eats and eats and eats,
trying to gain weight.
One afternoon he eats a shortcake,
then drinks a milk shake,
then thirteen ice-cream bars
and eleven bottles of pop.

As he gets older,
he keeps practicing.
He is always swinging something—
a bat, or a stick, or a pillow,
or a rolled-up newspaper.
He watches his swing in the mirror,
again and again and again.
Two on, two out, last of the ninth . . .

CHAPTER TWO

In 1935, his junior year in high school,
he hits .583 and leads his team
to the league championship.
Big-league scouts board trains in
New York, Detroit, and St. Louis
and travel all the way across America,
all the way to San Diego, California,
just to see Ted Williams hit.

The New York Yankees offer him a contract.
He is only seventeen years old,
too young to sign it himself.
His mother doesn't want him so far away,
so she rejects the Yankees' offer
and arranges to have him play
for the local minor-league team,
the San Diego Padres
of the Pacific Coast League.

He hasn't even graduated
from high school yet,
and Ted Williams is a
professional baseball player.

Riding on a train for the very first time,
in a special car just for ballplayers,
Ted Williams can't sit still.
He does fingertip push-ups beside his bunk
and swings and swings and swings.
Two on, two out, last of the ninth . . .

He is in heaven.
Almost every day, there is a game,
and a doubleheader every Sunday.
After games, while other players shower
and get dressed and play cards,
Ted Williams grabs a few baseballs
and pays a clubhouse kid
twenty-five cents to pitch to him.
He swings the bat until his hands bleed.

In December 1937,
after two seasons with the Padres,
nineteen-year-old Ted Williams
signs his first big-league contract,
with the Boston Red Sox.

CHAPTER THREE

Four years later,
Ted Williams is an all-star.

He steps up to the plate,
batting cleanup for the American League
in the 1941 Major League All-Star Game
at Briggs Stadium in Detroit.

Two on, two out,
last of the ninth,
down five to four,
two balls, one strike.
The pitcher winds up.
Ted Williams sees the ball.
He swings.

HOME RUN!

He circles the bases,
not running
but leaping, bouncing,
almost floating,
jumping up and down
and clapping his hands
and laughing
all the way to home plate.

Ted Williams is living his dream.
Still only twenty-two years old,
he might already be
the best hitter in baseball.

He hits and hits and hits.
He finishes 1941 with a
batting average of .406,
one of the finest seasons
a ballplayer has ever had.

But then everything changes.

CHAPTER FOUR

World War II has already begun.
Battles have been raging in faraway places.
But then on December 7,
Japan attacks the U.S. naval base
at Pearl Harbor.

America is at war.

In May 1942,
Ted Williams enlists in the
navy's V-5 training program.
He plays for the rest of the season and
wins the American League triple crown.
In November, he reports for duty and
begins training to become a fighter pilot.

He studies hard.
He learns about navigation,
aerodynamics, and math.
The classes are tough
at preliminary ground school.
Most cadets fail.
Ted Williams makes it all the way
to advanced pilot training.

He learns to fly.
He masters takeoffs, slow rolls, night flying,
inverted spins, and precision landings.
He sets a student gunnery record for aerial fire.

By the summer of 1945,
Second Lieutenant Ted Williams
is waiting for his orders
to join the battle in the Pacific.

Then, on September 2, 1945,
Japan officially surrenders.
World War II is over.
Ted Williams is going home.

CHAPTER FIVE

On Opening Day in 1946,
at Washington's Griffith Stadium,
President Truman watches
from the front row
as the Red Sox take on the Senators.
Second Lieutenant Ted Williams
steps into the batter's box.
It's been three years
since his last big-league game.

The pitcher winds up.
Ted Williams sees the ball.
He swings.

HOME RUN!

It lands in the bleachers,
four hundred and sixty feet away,
farther than anyone has ever hit
a ball in Griffith Stadium.

For the next six seasons,
he is golden.
He is back where he wants to be,
living his dream.
He is the greatest hitter in baseball.
In 1946, he leads the Red Sox
all the way to the World Series,
only to lose in seven games
to the St. Louis Cardinals.
In 1947, he wins the American League
triple crown for the second time.
He wins two Most Valuable Player awards.
He swings and swings and swings.

Then everything changes again.
The United States is at war again.
The marines need pilots.
On January 9, 1952,
Ted Williams gets a letter in the mail.

He is going to Korea.

If he makes it back safely,
he will be thirty-five when he returns.
Most ballplayers are done by thirty-five.

On April 30, 1952,
he plays what might be
his final game in the major leagues.
The mayor of Boston declares it
Ted Williams Day.

In the bottom of the seventh inning,
with the score tied three to three,
Ted Williams steps up to the plate
for what might be
the last at bat of his career.

The pitcher winds up.
Ted Williams sees the ball.
He swings.

CHAPTER SIX

Ten months later, on February 16, 1953,
Captain Ted Williams
is on his first combat mission,
blazing through the fog
in an F9F Panther fighter jet,
deep in enemy territory.

Suddenly, a red light turns on.
The whole plane starts shaking.
He tries to call for help,
but his radio is dead.

He has been hit.

If he ejects from the plane,
he could break both his legs.
If he breaks his legs,
he'll never play baseball again.

Ted Williams decides to crash.

Carefully, steadily,
he guides his broken plane
to an air force base near the front line.
His plane hits the landing strip
engulfed in flames,
going 225 miles per hour,
and skids for nine thousand feet.
Pieces of the plane break off.
Everything but the cockpit is on fire.

Finally it stops,
and Ted Williams jumps out.

He is okay.

CHAPTER SEVEN

On July 28, 1953,
after flying thirty-nine
combat missions in Korea,
Ted Williams is back in Boston.
He hasn't played baseball in over a year.
The ballpark is mostly empty.
The few people who are there—
ushers, hot-dog vendors,
ballplayers taking batting practice—
all stop what they are doing and watch.

Ted Williams is going to hit.

He steps into the cage.

For the first time in over a year,

he swings: line drive into right field.

He hits a few more line drives, and then . . .

BOOM! A home run!

Next pitch—**BOOM!**

And then another.

He swings and swings and swings.

He hits nine home runs in a row.

His hands crack,

not used to gripping a bat.

Blood runs down his knuckles.

He keeps swinging and swinging.

Ted Williams is home.

He rejoins the Red Sox in August
and bats .407 the rest of the season.
He hits thirteen home runs
in just thirty-seven games.
He is thirty-five years old now,
but Ted Williams is not done yet.

He plays seven more seasons.
He wins two more batting titles.
In 1957, at the age of thirty-nine,
he has one of the finest seasons
of his life, batting .388.
He is named the Major League Baseball
Player of the Decade for the 1950s.

CHAPTER EIGHT

On September 28, 1960,
at Fenway Park in Boston,
Ted Williams walks to the plate
for the final time.
He waits for over two minutes
for the crowd to stop cheering.
They do not stop.

Finally he steps into the batter's box.
He stands upright, knees slightly bent,
feet twenty-seven inches apart,
front foot twelve inches off the plate,
back foot dug into the dirt,
same as always.
The pitcher winds up.
Ted Williams sees the ball.
He swings.

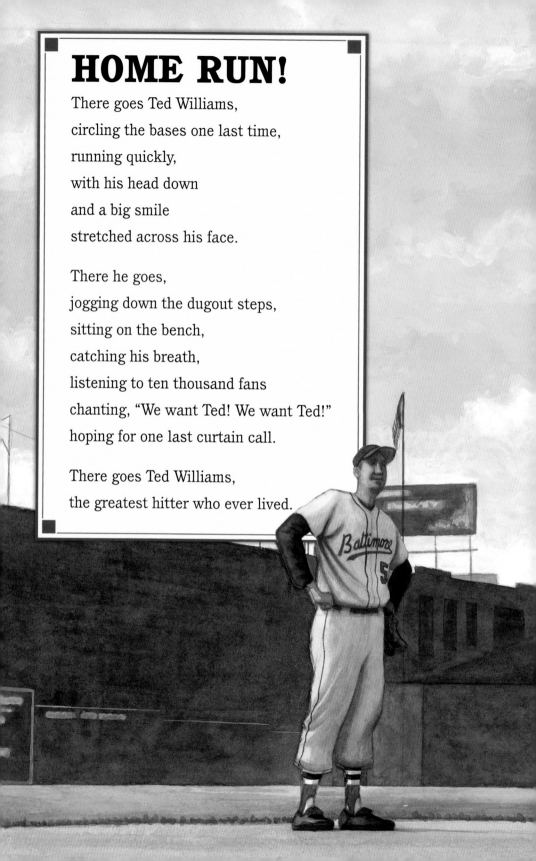

HOME RUN!

There goes Ted Williams,
circling the bases one last time,
running quickly,
with his head down
and a big smile
stretched across his face.

There he goes,
jogging down the dugout steps,
sitting on the bench,
catching his breath,
listening to ten thousand fans
chanting, "We want Ted! We want Ted!"
hoping for one last curtain call.

There goes Ted Williams,
the greatest hitter who ever lived.

AUTHOR'S NOTE

Ted Williams was my father's childhood idol. I grew up hearing stories about how high his home runs went, how the ball seemed to go straight up into the sky and just kept carrying until it cleared the fence. My father told me about the time a pitcher was intentionally walking Ted Williams but left one a little too close to the plate, and the great Ted Williams reached out and lined a double into left field. He took me to Fenway Park and showed me the one red seat in a sea of green seats, deep in the bleachers, impossibly far from home plate, that marks the spot where the ball landed when Ted Williams hit the longest home run in the history of Fenway Park. The Ted Williams I grew up with was larger than life. He could see the seams on a Bob Feller fastball. He could fly a fighter jet. He could do pretty much anything.

Researching his life, I learned that Ted Williams was far from perfect. He had a terrible temper. He swore too much. He threw tantrums. For most of his career, he was embroiled in a bitter feud with

the Boston fans and media. He hated sportswriters, and most of them hated him. Part of me did not want to know these things about Ted Williams.

But as I read more about him, something else struck me. Even with all his faults, the Ted Williams I heard about as a child was real, too. The high, towering home runs, his incredible .406 season, his unparalleled dedication to perfecting the art of hitting a baseball, the home run in his final at bat: it was all true. I even read some stories that were more amazing than the ones my father told me, like the time he hit nine consecutive home runs in an impromptu batting practice session during his first trip back to Fenway, just after flying thirty-nine combat missions in the Korean War.

I also learned about his lifelong dedication to helping sick children. During his career, he made countless unreported visits to the Jimmy Fund Clinic, not just stopping by to say hi but actually staying and spending time with kids, helping them with their homework, talking about hitting, promising home runs and brightening their worlds. He was the single most influential person in helping to raise money for the Dana Farber Cancer Institute, which still thrives today.

He was an ordinary kid who dreamed of being the greatest hitter who ever lived, then dedicated his life to making that dream come true. His story also shows the tremendous sacrifices that men and women of his generation made, risking all he had worked for to serve his country in two wars. The story of Ted Williams is the story of an American hero.

BIBLIOGRAPHY

Creamer, Robert W. *Baseball in '41.* New York: Viking, 1991.

Johnson, Dick, and Glenn Stout. *Ted Williams: A Portrait in Words and Pictures.* New York: Walker, 1991.

Linn, Ed. *Hitter: The Life and Turmoils of Ted Williams.* San Diego: Harcourt Brace, 1994.

Montville, Leigh. *Ted Williams: The Biography of an American Hero.* New York: Doubleday, 2004.

Nowlin, Bill. *Ted Williams at War.* Burlington, MA: Rounder Books, 2007.

Seidel, Michael. *Ted Williams: A Baseball Life.* 2nd ed. Lincoln, NE: University of Nebraska Press, 2000.

Williams, Ted, with John Underwood. *My Turn At Bat.* New York: Simon and Schuster, 1969.

——— with John Underwood. *The Science of Hitting.* New York: Simon and Schuster, 1971.

——— with David Pietrusza. *Ted Williams: My Life in Pictures.* Kingston, NY: Total/Sports Illustrated, 2001.

TED WILLIAMS

Height: 6 feet 3 inches; Weight: 205 lbs.; Born: San Diego, California

YEAR	TEAM	G	AB	R	H
1939	Red Sox	149	565	131	185
1940	Red Sox	144	561	**134**	193
1941	Red Sox	143	456	**135**	185
1942	Red Sox	150	522	**141**	186
1943					
1944	(Served in World War II)				
1945					
1946	Red Sox	150	514	**142**	176
1947	Red Sox	156	528	**125**	181
1948	Red Sox	137	509	124	188
1949	Red Sox	**155**	566	**150**	194
1950	Red Sox	89	334	82	106
1951	Red Sox	148	531	109	169
1952	Red Sox	6	10	2	4
1953	Red Sox	37	91	17	37
1954	Red Sox	117	386	93	133
1955	Red Sox	98	320	77	114
1956	Red Sox	136	400	71	138
1957	Red Sox	132	420	96	163
1958	Red Sox	129	411	81	135
1959	Red Sox	103	272	32	69
1960	Red Sox	113	310	56	98
MLB Career		2,292	7,706	1,798	2,654

Bold stats represent instances where Ted Williams led the league. From 1943 to 1945, Ted Williams served in World War II and did not play baseball. From 1952 to 1953, he played shortened seasons due to his service in the Korean War.

HR	RBI	BB	SO	BA	OBP	SLG
31	**145**	107	64	.327	.436	.609
23	113	96	54	.344	**.442**	.594
37	120	**147**	27	**.406**	**.553**	**.735**
36	**137**	**145**	51	**.356**	**.499**	**.648**
			(Served in World War II)			
38	123	**156**	44	.342	**.497**	**.667**
32	**114**	**162**	47	**.343**	**.499**	**.634**
25	127	**126**	41	**.369**	**.497**	**.615**
43	**159**	**162**	48	.343	**.490**	**.650**
28	97	82	21	.317	.452	.647
30	126	**144**	45	.318	**.464**	**.556**
1	3	2	2	.400	.500	.900
13	34	19	10	.407	.509	.901
29	89	**136**	32	.345	**.513**	**.635**
28	83	91	24	.356	.496	.703
24	82	102	39	.345	**.479**	.605
38	87	119	43	**.388**	**.526**	**.731**
26	85	98	49	**.328**	**.458**	.584
10	43	52	27	.254	.372	.419
29	72	75	41	.316	.451	.645
521	1,839	2,021	709	.344	.482	.634

Key: G = Games, AB = At Bats, R = Runs, H = Hits, HR = Home Runs, RBI = Runs Batted In, BB = Walks, SO = Strikeouts, BA = Batting Average, OBP = On Base Percentage, SLG = Slugging Percentage

INDEX

All-Star Game (1941), 8

American League, 8, 12, 18

batting average, 4, 11, 28

big leagues, 4, 7

Boston, 20, 26–27

Boston Red Sox. *See* Red Sox

Briggs Stadium, 8

Cardinals, 18

Dana Farber Cancer Institute, 34

Detroit, 8

doubleheaders, 7

Fenway Park, 30–33, 34

Griffith Stadium, 16

high school, 4

home runs, 1, 8, 16, 21, 27, 28, 32, 34

Jimmy Fund, 34

Korea, 18, 22–25, 26, 34

Major League Baseball, 8, 18, 28

minor leagues, 4

Most Valuable Player award, 18

Navy, U.S., 12–15

New York Yankees, 4

North Park playground, 1

Pacific Coast League, 4

Padres, 4, 7

plane crash, 22–24

Player of the Decade, 28

practices, 1, 3, 7

professional player, 4

Washington, D.C., 16

Washington Senators, 16

World Series (1946), 18

World War II, 12–15

Red Sox, 7, 16, 18, 28, 30–32

retirement, 30–32

Yankees, 4

San Diego, California, 1, 4

San Diego Padres, 4, 7

scouts, 4

Senators, 16

St. Louis Cardinals, 18

statistics, 36–37

Ted Williams Day, 20

triple crown, 12, 18

MATT TAVARES is the author-illustrator of *Zachary's Ball*, *Oliver's Game*, *Mudball*, *Becoming Babe Ruth*, and *Henry Aaron's Dream*, which was an Orbis Pictus Recommended Book. He is also the illustrator of *Iron Hans*, *'Twas the Night Before Christmas*, *Jack and the Beanstalk*, Doreen Rappaport's *Lady Liberty*, and Kristin Kladstrup's *The Gingerbread Pirates*. About *There Goes Ted Williams*, he says, "The Ted Williams I grew up hearing about seemed larger than life. He could see the seams on a Bob Feller fastball. He could fly a fighter jet. He could do just about anything. After researching his life and making this book, I'm every bit as amazed by Ted Williams as I have always been." Matt Tavares lives in Ogunquit, Maine.